"In a world of increasing confusion and shouted opinions, this book is full of solid, calm, dependable, simple, straight-talking truth. It will actually help you to reflect on who you are and what you were made for—giving answers that are both refreshingly simple and deeply satisfying."

ANDY ACHESON, Author, *Who Is God?*

"This book helps young people engage thoughtfully with a Christian worldview at a time when many of their assumptions are being tested. Shaped by the voices of youth workers and leaders who understand the realities young people face, it offers insight, honesty and lived experience. It creates space to wrestle with big questions, reflect deeply and consider what it means to live out faith in today's culture."

DAVE BODEN, Author, *Raising Gen Alpha* and *Like or Follow*

HOW TO BE HUMAN

12 Truths to Build Your Life On

EDITED BY
Andrew Wilson

How to Be Human

Published by:
The Good Book Company

thegoodbook.com | thegoodbook.co.uk
thegoodbook.com.au | thegoodbook.co.nz

Every book published by The Good Book Company has been written by a human author and edited by a human editor. While AI tools are sometimes used to assist with research and support certain processes, all content has been created by a human author and thoroughly checked by our editorial team to ensure it is biblically faithful and pastorally wise.

Titles published by The Good Book Company may be purchased in bulk for educational, business, fundraising or sales promotional use. For information and bespoke pricing, please email SpecialMarkets@thegoodbook.com.

Cover design by André Parker

ISBN: 9781802544534 | JOB-008820 | Printed in Turkey

Contents

Introduction

ANDREW WILSON

Being human is the greatest privilege a creature can have. You are at the top of the food chain. You have a large brain, an upright spine and opposable thumbs. You can talk, read, imagine, create and worship. Most importantly, you have been created in the image of God. You are an icon: a picture of God for all the world to see.

But that privilege brings challenges. It always has. With great power comes great responsibility, as Uncle Ben so famously said to Spiderman. Human beings have the capacity to do magnificent good or spectacular harm. We can discover penicillin, or invent atom bombs; our speech can bring life, or it can bring destruction; we can lead people into the heavenly presence of God, or hellish rebellion. So, if we are going to be life-givers rather than destroyers, we need to know how to handle our humanity well.

That is complicated in this generation. We spend more of our time looking at screens than faces. Isolation is on the rise. Artificial intelligence is already having an impact on the way we learn and the jobs we will do. There has never been a more important time for us to know how to be human.

And that's what this book is about. It gives you twelve truths to live by, drawn from the most important thing that has ever been written about being human: the first three chapters of Genesis, the first book of the Bible. You will learn about God and creation; what it means to be made in his image as male and female; God's intentions for work, sex and marriage; and how to think about the problems of sin and suffering, and God's wonderful response in the gospel.

If you're a Christian, not a Christian, or not sure, this book is for you. Read it and see what you think about the Bible's take on how to be human.

CHAPTER 1: GOD

The God of eternity invites you to know him.

STU GIBBS

The Bible starts simply, doesn't it? "In the beginning God..." It doesn't try to define God or explain him. It just places him at the centre and beginning of all things. *In the beginning, God.* That's the starting point of everything we know.

When you're used to talking about God, it's easy to take him for granted. Between the ages of 0 and 18, I went to church pretty much every week. If you count youth group meetings on Friday nights as well, that's over a thousand church meetings before I was an adult. I knew a fair amount about God... but I didn't know God. Not really.

I only recognised this when I went to a Christian event and met a bunch of people who did. They seemed eager to pray, passionate about worship and fascinated by the Bible. I suddenly had a deep hunger to find out more. I realised that God was not just real but *knowable*—and so the best and most important thing in life would be to know him as he really is.

Genesis 1 sets us off on that journey: "In the beginning God..." These first few verses don't tell us everything that can be known about God, but they do point us in the direction of some pretty major truths. Life-changing truths, even.

God Is Eternal

What counts as a long time ago for you? Before the Covid lockdown? England winning the World Cup in 1966? The Egyptians building the pyramids around 2,500 BC? How about the moment the sun was formed? God was present for each one of those events, as well as every other event in history. In the beginning—when God began history as we know it—*he had already been present for ever.*

This is pretty mind-blowing. You should try to keep thinking about it, because it will stop you thinking about God as if he is an older and wiser version of you.

It means that there was never a time when he wasn't. He didn't develop into God over time and eventually reach perfection. However many trillions of years you go back, he was already present, perfect and glorious.

It means he has no cause. Nothing else came before him, gave birth to him or produced him. He is the cause of everything that exists, and he isn't dependent on anything else.

It means he is unchanging: "the same yesterday and today and for ever" (Hebrews 13:8). Everything else changes, but God never does. He is permanent in his perfect wisdom, power, love and glory.

This is why God revealed himself in a flaming fire to Moses and said, "I AM WHO I AM" (Exodus 3:14). We don't get to decide who he is, what he is like or what he should do. But—and this is important—we do get invited to listen to him as he reveals himself to us. And what the eternal God shows us about himself is more profound and marvellous than we could ever have guessed.

God Is Three in One

In Genesis 1, God shows up straight away and is described as the Creator of all things. We also read that the Spirit of God is hovering over the waters, ready for action (1:2). And then we find that creation happens as God speaks: "Let there be light!" *Boom!* "And there was light." So the Bible describes God creating by his word, through his Spirit. There is one God, but he's also more than one.

When we get near the end of the chapter, God drops in another clue: "Let *us* make mankind in our image" (v 26). "Us"? Who is he talking about? All the way through the Bible, God keeps up the hints—until the moment of revelation finally arrives with the coming of Jesus. John's Gospel explains the mystery: "In the beginning was the Word, and the Word was with God, and the Word was God" (John 1:1). God was not on his own; the Word was with him. Then "the Word became flesh and made his dwelling among us" (John 1:14).

Christians are baptised "in the name of the Father, the Son and the Holy Spirit", because one God exists in three Persons. We use the word "Trinity" (Tri-unity) to describe this. Over the years people have tried all kinds of ways to explain this three-in-one God: eggs, triangles, water-ice-steam, and pretty much anything that connects three and one together. None of them quite work, and you know you've definitely taken a wrong turn if you end up picturing God as an enormous triangular egg who can shape-shift into a liquid or a gas.

The Trinity *is* just hard to wrap your mind around—and that's okay. After all, God is the infinite Creator, and we are his creatures. When my kids were toddlers, they could understand that they had parents who loved and looked after them before they could say ma-ma or da-da, and certainly before they understood what marriage or family was! For us, it's enough to know that we have a heavenly Father who loves us, a Saviour who died for us, and the Holy Spirit who breathes life into us, even if we don't yet have a clue how that is supposed to work.

But understanding God as the Trinity is not just good for scoring points in a theology test; it helps us to understand something crucial. Nabeel Qureshi was a Muslim who converted to Christianity after years of study. At first he was embarrassed and awkward about the Trinity as it confused his friends, and so he avoided talking about it. Over time, though, he began to make it the first thing he described in conversations about God. Why? Because he concluded that it pointed to the most incredible truth about what God is like. Which is...

God Overflows with Goodness

In John 17, we get to overhear Jesus praying to his Father. "Father," he asks, "I want those you have given me to ... see my glory, the glory you have given me because you loved me before the creation of the world" (John 17:24). Wow. You might have seen sports stars pause their celebrations and bring their kids onto the pitch to share the moment. This prayer shows us that the heart of Jesus is to draw *us* in to share in the love and glory that he has enjoyed with the Father and the Spirit for all eternity.

That's why God created the world. That's why God sent his Son. That's why God's Spirit is still present and active, drawing people like you and me into faith and friendship with our Father. It's because God is love and has been for ever. God didn't create the world because he was bored with Jesus and wanted someone else to talk to. Creation was the overflow of his goodness so that people like you and me could join in and share the love and glory he has always had.

God spoke, and created a world full of rich blessings—stars and seas, food and friendship, love and laughter—so that through it we could taste and see his overflowing goodness. And even though we rebelled against him and went our own way (more on that in later chapters), that wasn't the end of the story. God has poured out his love, Jesus came and poured out his life, the Holy Spirit continues to be poured out on God's people, and we are invited to freely receive all God's blessings.

How to Know God

You could spend your whole life studying the nature of God and never run out of things to think about. In fact, everyone who belongs to Jesus will spend eternity knowing and enjoying him. Right now, though, I would encourage you to do one thing that will help you build a relationship with God based on these beautiful truths: pray.

Most of us find it hard to pray. We may not know what to say. It might feel weird talking to someone you can't see. But I've learnt over the years that it helps to remember who we are praying to before we start. Sometimes I think about God's eternal nature, which reminds me of how much wiser and stronger he is than me. Or I think about the love and glory that has always been his, and Christ's prayer that we would share in it. I might list some of the blessings he has poured out, and try to let his goodness sink into my heart. It makes a big difference to my experience of being in his presence, and to the kind of prayers I pray.

Since I went to that festival aged 18, I've been to church a lot more times—but now I do it as someone who knows God. I've found comfort, peace, joy, truth and wisdom in knowing him that is far better than anything I've found elsewhere. The God of eternity invites me in, and I say yes. What about you?

"I would say that because I know God, I feel happier. I feel like I'm not weighed down—the burden of sin has been taken off my back. It's not that I don't struggle, but I have a comfort in Jesus that I can rejoice in."

OLLIE, AGED 16

CHAPTER 2: CREATION

The universe demands an explanation.

ADRIAN HOLLOWAY

Imagine you go walking in a forest with your friends and you come across a ball on the ground. You wonder aloud how it got there. One friend says, "Oh, that ball has always been there." Another friend says, "There is no explanation. Nobody made it or put it there. It just is."

Now imagine the ball is much bigger. Imagine it is the size of a football stadium. Or imagine the ball is as big as our universe. How would you feel about the friend who says that the ball exists for no reason at all?

I think we would all find that hard to accept. I think we'd feel that something as big as the universe demands some sort of explanation.

According to Genesis, that explanation is that God created the world (1:1-2). God formed the universe, separating light and dark (v 3-5), sea and sky (v 6-8), and land and water (v 9-10). And he filled the universe—with plants (v 11-13), stars (v 14-19), fish and birds (v 20-23), animals (v 24-25) and finally humans (v 26-31).

And the more you look into scientific findings about the origins of the cosmos, the more convincing this simple explanation seems. God created everything.

The Scientists Say...

Until a century ago, atheists used to argue that the universe is eternal. "Just accept it," they said. "It has always been there." They argued that the universe was locked in a permanent, stable "steady state".

Then, in 1929, an astronomer called Edwin Hubble took a series of photos which suggested that the universe is not locked in a steady state at all—rather, it is expanding. Picture the universe as a black balloon covered in white stars and galaxies. What Hubble realised is that the galaxies are moving away from each other, as if the balloon is being blown up. The universe is not static. It is expanding.

By the 1960s, cosmologists were broadly agreed that since the universe is expanding, it must have once been much smaller than it is now. And before that, they concluded, the universe must have had a beginning. Then, in 1965, astronomers Robert Wilson and Arno Penzias discovered some background radiation in the universe that was left behind by this "beginning" moment (which today we call the Big Bang). The radiation is like a signature left behind by this beginning.

As a result, there is now scientific agreement that at one time, the universe began. That is a profound discovery. It is not that matter and energy suddenly increased within a space-time universe that already existed. It is that space, time and energy themselves began to exist at this beginning moment! Our universe suddenly came into existence out of nothing.

Here is another way of thinking about it. If the universe has existed for ever, it should have run out of energy by now. The second law of thermodynamics states that disorder always increases—you can scramble an egg, but you can't unscramble it—and heat and energy are continually being lost. If the universe has existed for ever, then all the order in the universe should have dissolved by now—just as, if you lost your phone down the back of the sofa and found it ten years later, you would expect it to have run out of battery.

But the universe hasn't. There is actually *more* complexity and order in the universe now than there was to start with, from eyeballs to iPhones. (Notice that increasing complexity is also the trajectory in Genesis 1.) This suggests that the universe must have had a beginning.

The Search for a Cause

If it is true that the universe began to exist, then it is very plausible to think that it was created by someone. The logic here is simple:

1. Everything that begins to exist has a cause.
2. The universe began to exist.
3. Therefore the universe has a cause.

We've already seen that step #2 is generally accepted by scientists today. As for step #1, you don't need to be a scientist to be confident that it's reasonable. We certainly don't know of any exceptions to it.

If the universe came into existence uncaused, then why don't other things do the same? Why doesn't an elephant pop into existence uncaused when you're brushing your teeth in the bathroom? What is so special about universes that it means they can exist without a cause, whereas cars, trains and zebras never do? To say that the universe came into being *without* a cause is more irrational than believing in magic. When a magician pulls a rabbit out of a hat, at least you've got the hat, and indeed the magician. There's certainly a cause; you just don't know how it works. But to believe that the rabbit appears uncaused? That's just silly.

If steps #1 and #2 are true, then step #3 must be too. Something (or Someone) caused the universe to come into being. And a cause that is capable of bringing space, time, matter and energy into existence—well, you could call that first cause "God".

This Improbable World

If you still need convincing, consider the fine-tuning of the universe. Scientists have observed that if the set-up of the cosmos were just very slightly different, we wouldn't exist.

For example, we know that if we were a little bit closer to the sun, we'd fry, and if we were just a little bit further away, we'd freeze. There would be no life on earth. We also know that our solar system just happens to be in what astronomers call "the Goldilocks zone" of our Milky Way, a specific area where a whole series of surprising features makes complex life possible.

But the degree of fine-tuning that we're talking about with the origin of the universe is far more impressive than any of that. Scientific models suggest that at the beginning of the universe, when matter began flying outwards, it had to move at a very specific speed. Too fast and matter would not have been able to hold together. Too slow and the universe would have collapsed in on itself. Now get this: if the rate of expansion one second after the beginning of the universe had been smaller by one part in a hundred thousand million million, the universe would have re-collapsed before planets could emerge, let alone the arrival of people.

The point? Our existence is utterly improbable, and yet here we are. It's hard not to conclude that someone deliberately set the universe up this way.

These examples are just the start. Sir Roger Penrose, who helped develop our current understanding of black holes, worked out the probability of the level of disorder (or entropy) at the start of the universe being what it was. He calculated that it was one chance in 10 to the power of 10 to the power of 123. Sorry if you don't like maths—but perhaps it's enough to say that the larger the number is at the end of a phrase like "one chance in ten", the more unlikely the thing is to happen. And that number I just mentioned has more zeros on the end of it than the total number of particles in the entire universe.

There are plenty of other numbers, too, which have to be precise. Gravity and electromagnetism have to be fine-tuned to each other, or no complex life would exist. The same is true of matter and anti-matter, neutrons and electrons, the strong and weak nuclear forces, and so on. Any messing with these numbers and there would be no world as we know it.

A Plausible Explanation

We could go on—there are many other arguments and pieces of evidence for a Creator that there is no space for here.

But for me, eventually, I came to the conclusion that in any other area of my life, I would never accept sheer luck or chance as an explanation for facts like these. So why should I accept such an explanation for the universe? The verdict given in Genesis—that God created the world—seems far more plausible.

People take different views on how exactly to interpret the story of how God brought about the development of life on earth—for example, did it really happen in seven days? It's worthwhile exploring those questions. But don't miss this most fundamental point: the opening line of Genesis is a reasonable and respectable explanation for the existence of the amazing universe we see around us. "In the beginning God created the heavens and the earth."

"I have had so many life experiences that I just simply cannot explain with any answer other than God working miracles. That's what made me give my life to Christ."

DAN, AGED 18

CHAPTER 3: IMAGE

Human beings are designed to be like God.

TAYLOR BENTLIFF

What do you want to do with your life? Over the years, I've wanted to be a tennis player, gymnast, data analyst, Broadway star, interpreter, chef and journalist. In my defence, it can often feel like there are too many options! And for most of us, there are times in life when we have absolutely no idea what we're made for.

What does it mean to be a human, and to do it well? The first chapter of Genesis gives us what might feel like a surprising nudge in the right direction...

Human beings are unique. All of God's creation is "good", but it is only after he creates humans that God says it is "very good" (Genesis 1:31). Why? Because unlike anything else in the universe, we were designed to bear the image of our Creator.

> "So God created mankind in his own image, in the image of God he created them; male and female he created them." (Genesis 1:27)

Bearing God's image means we carry the likeness of who God is. We share important aspects of his divine character: spirituality, morality, community, creativity, authority and responsibility.

Understanding those characteristics might change the whole way we think about ourselves and what we're here for.

Humans Are Spiritual

> "Then the LORD God formed a man from the dust of the ground and breathed into his nostrils the breath of life, and the man became a living being." (2:7)

It's easy to assume that this verse is simply about God providing Adam with oxygen. But there is more going on here. God is a spiritual being, so he doesn't possess lungs or need air in the same way we do. This verse is saying that humans have the same kind of life, the same kind of spirit, that God has. We are spiritual, not just physical. We are heavenly, not just earthly.

That is why every human being has unimaginable value. That is why every human life—whatever our age, sex or race, and however small or incapable we are—is sacred. This basic truth is foundational to human rights; it is why people in cultures influenced by Christianity believe in opposing corrupt leadership, protecting the vulnerable and grieving injustice. It is why every single person on the planet should be valued and shown dignity. Just imagine what the world would be like if everyone really did see each fellow human as a reflection of our Creator!

Humans Are Moral

Are humans basically good or bad? I used to think that Adam and Eve were the only humans who ever truly resembled God and his goodness, and that as soon as sin came into the world, the "image of God" was ripped from us and we became fundamentally bad. But actually it's more complicated than that. All of us *are* made in the image of God; all of us *do* fall short of the image of God; and as we follow Jesus, all of us are being transformed into the image of God.

Imagine that when God made humans, he created a beautiful jigsaw puzzle. The picture on the box shows what's inside: a person who reflects God's perfect character, with no pieces missing and everything fitting perfectly—*very* good. But, starting with Adam and continuing through every generation, our rebellion against God has spoiled the jigsaw. Pieces have faded and come unstuck. Sometimes it is hard to recognise the original image at all.

But when we follow Jesus, the perfect image of the invisible God, he restores the jigsaw. Piece by piece, he builds us back together to display his image more and more clearly. One Bible writer puts it like this: "[We] have put on the new self, which is being renewed in knowledge in the image of its Creator" (Colossians 3:10). With Jesus, no matter what we've done, we are on a path back towards being "very good". The truth is, we have all fallen short of reflecting God's "very good" image—but through Jesus we can be restored without shame.

Humans Belong in Community

God is all about relationships. We see it in his very nature: Father, Son and Holy Spirit. And when God comes to earth in person, in Jesus, we see how committed he is to community. Jesus had lots of friends. He shared experiences, meals and challenges with people in community, including those who were normally marginalised. Much of his teaching described how we should love and honour others. And ultimately, Jesus came to restore the broken relationship between humans and God. We can be sure that God loves relationship.

Genesis makes this crystal clear. God gives Adam his very breath (2:7), talks to him (2:16) and walks with him in the garden (3:8). When he looks at Adam, he declares that "it is not good for man to be alone" (2:18) and makes him a partner, Eve. God created us male and female so we could resemble him in relationship and community.

Throughout the Bible we see God invite generations of people, of all ages and nationalities, with different interests and characteristics, to be in relationship with him and one another. Whether you have found your tribe or have struggled to connect with others, Jesus wants you to be an important part of his great family, the church. Everyone is invited.

Humans Are Creative

God is undeniably creative. He could have made a boring planet filled with boring creatures and boring people. He could have left the sky blank and provided one type of food or weather that never changes (although, being British, to me that doesn't sound all that bad!). Instead, God spoke and created a world of colour, excitement and creativity.

Once creation was complete, God immediately told Adam to exercise his own creativity by naming all the animals:

> "Now the LORD God had formed out of the ground all the wild animals and all the birds in the sky. He brought them to the man to see what he would name them; and whatever the man called each living creature, that was its name." (2:19)

Isn't that amazing? Adam bears God's image, so he imitates his Creator, speaking words over creation and establishing rules for it to follow. Adam is invited by God to get involved—and we follow in his footsteps. Humans are speakers, dreamers, designers, artists, builders. We invent systems, organise day trips and discuss new ideas. We were created to create: to bring order to chaos and light in the darkness, just like the God whose image we bear.

Humans Have Authority

I have a one-year-old daughter. She likes to be in control. She points directly at the book she wants to read, tidies up by throwing toys aggressively into the toy box, and manically shakes her head if presented with the wrong breadstick. (Apparently there is a *right* breadstick.) She moves as if she's in charge.

This becomes less charming when she decides to eat Blu Tack or pick up dog poo with her bare hands. She needs all kinds of help, correction and training. But fundamentally, her desire to rule the world reflects God's image. Look at Genesis again:

> "Fill the earth and subdue it. Rule over the fish in the sea and the birds in the sky and over every living creature that moves on the ground." (1:28)

Humans are created to rule the world on God's behalf. Like me with my daughter, God has to correct us and train us when we are disobedient, defiant and destructive. But he also loves to partner with us as we bring about goodness and order, in imitation of him. Image-bearers are kings and queens. And he made us that way.

Humans Are Responsible

Authority does not mean freedom to do whatever we want with creation. Yes, we are called to subdue and have dominion (1:28)—but the man was also put in the garden "to work it and take care of it" (2:15). Image-bearers have responsibility. God wants us to care for his world.

We've all had to work at something we don't really care about. I remember spending weeks in Design and Technology lessons at school, slaving over what eventually became a 5-out-of-10 wonky birdhouse. There were splinters, near misses with a saw and a wood glue that smelt of cat wee and ruined your clothes. I had no desire to build the birdhouse, look after it or enjoy it. I gave it to my mum—who honestly might have put it in the bin—and moved on without a second thought.

This is the opposite of God's heart towards his creation. He cares. He is deeply invested in it. He rules the world not by trashing or exploiting it but by taking responsibility for it—even facing death on a cross.

We take responsibility too. If you long to make the world a better place—whether in regard to the natural world or your fellow humans—that's because you've been created that way. It satisfies our soul when we successfully care for the things and people around us.

Humans were built different. We were created to signpost to our heavenly Father. My hope is that through exploring these characteristics, we can see more of God's heart shining through others, and ourselves! The next time you look in the mirror, remember, you have the opportunity to reflect the character of God to those around you. What a privilege!

CHAPTER 4: MALE

Being a man isn't something you earn but something you're given.

ANDREW WILSON

What does it take to be a real man?

It's a very pointed question, isn't it? I was at a men's conference a few years ago when one of the speakers put this to his audience. Sometimes speakers ask things like this and then immediately give their own answer straight away. But this one didn't. He got people talking, and waited for suggestions.

I don't know what you would have said in that moment. What does it take to be a real man? A girlfriend? A job? A beard? A family? A father who is proud of you? The ability to benchpress a certain weight, or speak up for yourself in a crowd, or drink alcohol, or fix a machine, or make a fire? What would you say?

The speaker listened carefully to all the responses and then gave his own answer. "Do you want to know what it takes to be a real man?" he asked. "It takes one thing, and one thing only. This is one of the most liberating things you will ever hear." The audience was on tenterhooks. "You are a real man... if you have (wait for it)... a penis."

There is so much confusion today about being male, manly or masculine. That's why the speaker said what he did. Some people think that being a "real man" is an achievement, when actually it is just a biological fact. Some people think masculinity is toxic: poisonous, harmful, destructive to men and dangerous to women. Some people say that, yes, masculinity involves strength and aggression and power—and we should use that strength to fight enemies, get girls, overpower weaker men, make money and establish dominance. Some people go completely the other way and deny that there is any fundamental difference between boys and girls or between men and women. Forget your biology, they say, and follow your feelings. You can be whoever and whatever you want to be.

They are all wrong. This is what God reveals to us in Genesis:

- Maleness is created, not achieved. It is given, not earned.
- Masculinity is good, healing and beneficial, not bad, toxic and destructive (although, like all of God's gifts, it can be abused).
- Men are not superior to women, and we are not inferior either; the two sexes are different but complementary.
- The strength that men are given by God is for service and protection, not oppression or dominance.
- Maleness is a biological reality, not a personal preference or social performance. It shapes everything about us.

Read those points again. How do they sound to you? Before you decide, look at these four key verses in Genesis 1 – 2 to see why these things are true.

Humans Are Made in God's Image

> "So God created man in his own image, in the image of God he created him; male and female he created them. And God blessed them. And God said to them, 'Be fruitful and multiply and fill the earth and subdue it and have dominion...'" (1:27-28, ESV)

All humans, whether male or female, are created in the image of God. You've looked at this verse already in this book, because it is absolutely crucial. Both men and women represent God on earth; the rest of creation can look at us and see something of what God is like. And both men and women are sent into the world with a commission: both to fill it with life ("be fruitful and multiply and fill") and to rule it wisely ("subdue it and have dominion"). The two sexes were designed to govern the world together. Neither is superior or inferior to the other. Being male does not make you better than a woman, and it does not make you worse.

Every generation sees this truth attacked in different ways. Many in history have believed that men can rule the world without women. Today, many talk as if women can fill the earth without men. But the word of God could not be clearer. God's image and God's commission belong to all humans, male and female.

Men and Women Have Different Origin Stories

> "The LORD God formed the man of dust from the ground and breathed into his nostrils the breath of life, and the man became a living creature." (2:7, ESV)

Notice the beautiful intimacy here. God first forms the man out of the soil and then breathes life into his nostrils to make him a living soul. The text presents God as a potter, fashioning clay and then filling the pot with the liquid he designed it to carry. Or we might think of a craftsman making a magnificent violin out of wood and then playing it for the first time so that it becomes a living instrument. We are dust *and* breath, body *and* soul, instrument *and* music.

Notice too the difference between the man and the woman. The man is formed from the ground, whereas the woman is formed from the side of the man. The man's origin story points to his responsibility for keeping the garden; the name "Adam" comes from the word for "ground" (*adamah*). The woman's origin story points to her responsibility for life; the name "Eve" comes from the word for "living" (*havah*). They're different—which means they will sometimes play different parts and do different things. But as we will see, neither the man nor the woman can fulfil these responsibilities without the other one.

The Man Has a Job to Do

> "The LORD God took the man and put him in the garden of Eden to work it and keep it."
> (2:15, ESV)

Now it gets interesting. For the first time, the man is given a task that is specifically his: to "work" and "keep" the garden. Try not to imagine pensioners pottering about with their flower beds here. This mountainous landscape called Eden is the source of four rivers, and it is covered in trees and full of minerals (2:8-14), so it's closer to a national park than a lawn. Looking after it involves hard work and vigilance, because (as we find out in Genesis 3) there are dangers and threats out there. That explains the two things God calls the man to do. The first is to "work, serve, labour." The second is to "guard, keep, watch over, protect." The man is meant to be a servant and a guardian.

That really matters. It makes sense of why the man would be held responsible for the serpent entering the garden; it was his job to protect it. It makes sense of why priests in the Old Testament had to be men; they were the ones charged with serving and guarding the Holy Place. It makes sense of why God created men to be on average bigger and stronger and with a higher appetite for risk than women. It makes sense of the different games that tend to be played by little girls and boys, and of the protectiveness men often feel towards others—and of the damage done when men choose not to be servants, not to be guardians, or both. It also pointed forward to the way the ultimate man, the Lord Jesus, became a servant to his people, laying down his life to protect them.

The Man Needs the Woman

> "Then the LORD God said, 'It is not good that the man should be alone; I will make him a helper fit for him.'" (2:18, ESV)

Just before we get carried away with how valuable and heroic men are, and start seeing ourselves as lone rangers who fight off bad guys single-handedly, the passage brings us back to reality. It is not good that the man should be alone, God says. There are lots of things he cannot do on his own. He needs a helper. He needs company, community, companionship, collaboration. He needs a woman.

This verse is often misunderstood to mean that it is not good for people to be single. But it does not mean that at all. (Jesus was single!) Men do not need marriage to thrive. But we do need community;

people who live "alone", in isolation from other humans, quickly unravel. And we do specifically need women (as wives but also as sisters, friends and co-workers), for all sorts of reasons that will emerge in the next chapter.

What it Takes to Be a Man

Brothers (and sisters): being a real man is not something earned, but something created. It is not the finishing line that you reach if you fulfil certain stereotypes. It is the starting line, and if you are male, you have been qualified for it by the God who created your sexual organs, the testosterone in your brain, and every XY cell in your body. God has given you his image, his commission, his breath in your nostrils and a mandate to serve and protect. The question is: what will you do with them?

CHAPTER 5: FEMALE

God created every woman on purpose, for a purpose.

KATHERINE BROWN

We shook hands. I introduced myself. She did a double take: “Oh, sorry! I didn’t think your voice was going to be that low.”

I laughed it off, as you do, but quickly texted some friends for reassurance. They said what friends say: *No, your voice is not that low. She probably just misheard you.* Maybe. But I couldn’t stop thinking about it.

Like you, I grew up in a world very much shaped by the feminist movement of the 1970s, which sought to break stereotypes and redefine the boundaries of womanhood. I also grew up an atheist, outside of the church, in a very female household. I was told that to be a woman was to be strong, independent, free; I could define womanhood however I liked. Yet despite being raised in that environment, when I was told my voice was low, I heard it as being called less of a woman. Perhaps you've had times like this too, when you've felt like you don't measure up.

Many stereotypes about femininity are narrow and unhelpful. When they are, we should challenge them. But many of the solutions offered in our culture aren't deep enough. We have replaced stereotypes with shallow platitudes: you do you, live your truth, you go girl. Being told that you can define your womanhood yourself, or your identity more generally, can sound freeing—until you realise that there are endless possibilities as to what this could mean, and no one to tell you what's right and what's not. It's hard to feel at peace with yourself when you face the constant pressure of self-creation. We find ourselves on shaky foundations.

That's why politicians and public figures squirm when asked the very simple question: what is a woman? Many reply that womanhood is something people choose because they identify with it. But that raises more questions. What if I haven't always naturally fitted into female stereotypes or sometimes do not feel woman enough? Am I less of a woman in those moments of insecurity? Am I closer to being a man or to something in between? Instead of the freedom we were promised, many of us feel less certain and more anxious about who we are and what we're meant to be doing.

Thankfully, God does not stumble over his words when defining what a woman is. The Bible gives us a beautifully empowering and honouring answer to this question, and provides the deeper, richer understanding we long for. Genesis 1 gives us the foundations; it's our starting point for learning how we can all flourish.

Woman as Image-Bearer

At the very start of the Bible, God creates men and women in his image.

> "So God created mankind in his own image, in the image of God he created them; male and female he created them." (1:27)

In this moment, we all receive our identity. Women, alongside men, are created in God's image. What does that mean? It means we reflect who God is to the world around us. This gives women immense value, because without women, God would not be imaged properly to the watching world. Women are undeniably different to men, but we equally bear the image of our Creator.

In God's eyes, the answer to the question of what it means to be a woman is clear. If he made you a woman, you are a woman. Your womanhood isn't a feeling, or a personality trait, or a set of stereotypes, or something you must define, earn or create yourself. You receive it as you're knitted together in your mother's womb (Psalm 139:13-14). Do you realise that?

Woman as Ruler and Helper

God then speaks to both men and women and tells them what their purpose is:

> "Be fruitful and increase in number; fill the earth and subdue it. Rule over the fish in the sea and the birds in the sky and over every living creature that moves on the ground."
>
> (Genesis 1:28)

Women aren't told to sit on the sidelines, cheering the men on. God says to both men and women, *Be fruitful, subdue the earth, and rule over creation.* Women aren't add-ons or spare parts. We are essential.

At this point, if you've read Genesis 1 – 3 before, you may be wondering about the word "helper", which is used to describe the woman a little later:

> "It is not good for the man to be alone. I will make a helper suitable for him." (2:18)

Doesn't that imply that women are inferior? I used to think so. I recoiled at the idea of being called a helper, partly because I'm a flawed, proud human—but also because I'd misunderstood how the Bible uses the word.

The Hebrew word for "helper" here, *ezer*, is used 21 times in Scripture. Guess who it refers to in 16 of those cases? God. That's right. God is our *ezer*, our helper, and that means this word cannot mean an inferior, weak or second-class role. Women are not here to watch the action unfold and maybe occasionally lend a hand. We are called to be active participants in the mission of God, with all our different gifts, personalities, strengths and quirks.

But how could Eve rule over creation and yet be called a helper? Surely it had to be one or the other? The feminist movement loved the idea that woman was a ruler but hated the idea that she was a helper. The manosphere does the opposite, insisting that women are helpers but not rulers. Scripture, by contrast, gives us a better vision: a fuller, more rounded one. A woman is both helper and ruler, both companion and queen. She supports, and she has dominion. That's what a woman is for.

Woman as Life-Bringer

But that is not all. We have already seen that the woman is called to be fruitful (1:28); as we read on in the story, she is given the name Eve, which means "life" or "living". And the reason for that is made clear: "because she would become the mother of all the living" (3:20). A woman is a life-bringer.

In Eve's case, that happened through having babies. But that isn't the only way women act as life-givers. Plenty of women in Scripture bring life to God's people without babies having anything to do with it. Miriam does it through her courage and her prophetic leadership. Deborah is a "mother in Israel", not by having children but because she serves as a judge and a prophet who summons the nation to fight (Judges 5:7). The New Testament is full of prominent women—Anna, Susanna, Mary and Martha, Mary Magdalene, Lydia, Priscilla, Phoebe, Philip's daughters, Chloe and others—who have no children mentioned and who bring life to God's people in a wide variety of ways: prophesying, teaching, giving, hosting, proclaiming the resurrection, serving as deacons and so on.

For some women, having children won't be their reality, whether through the pain of infertility or because of singleness and celibacy. But they are still life-bringers. Notice that Eve was named "life" before she had any babies.

The main emphasis of Eve's life-giving is that she starts off the generational line from which the ultimate life-giver, Jesus, will come. (More on this in chapters 9 and 11.) She will play her part in bringing forth the gospel. And that is what all women are created to do. We are those who bring life through the gospel to the people and places around us. We are those who make Jesus known: who carry him, as Mary did, to everyone around us.

The Purpose of a Woman

God made every woman to be unique, knitting us together in our mother's womb with care. He created us on purpose, for a purpose, with all our different quirks, habits and appearances. However we look. However we sound. Whatever we wear. Whether your voice is squeaky high or an octave lower than mine, and whether you feel more comfortable in football shirts or dresses, all these personality differences can be used for God's glory and for his kingdom.

Being a woman isn't a rigid set of traits, likes and dislikes. It's much deeper, much richer, much more profound than that. If God made you female, you get to join the countless women over history who have sat at the feet of Jesus, learning from him, giving their all to him and taking every opportunity to share the gospel and see God's kingdom come.

"We constantly compare our body, clothes, routine and life to strangers. It's crazy, but it can feel like an impossible loop to get out of. For me, knowing God is what has allowed me to step into confidence. I've been completely transformed."

GRACE, AGED 19

CHAPTER 6: WORK

work is meaningful because God calls us to it.

MBONISI MALABA

"Thank God it's Friday!" People often say this to express two things: relief that a school or work week is ending, and excitement at the prospect of a weekend of rest, relaxation and fun. While this makes a lot of sense, it's also just a little bit sad.

Think about it. From age 18 to 65 you're alive for just over 400,000 hours. You will be asleep for about one-third of those, which leaves about 250,000 hours of being awake. The average person will spend 4,000 hours on the toilet, 2,500 hours making love, 15,000 hours on holiday, and close to 50,000 hours... working.

Work is a big part of life. You would hope that the God who created us in his image, male and female, would have something to say about it. And thankfully he does.

Rest Is Good

Genesis 2 teaches us lots about work, but it starts by telling us about rest.

> "God blessed the seventh day and made it holy, because on it he rested from all the work of creating that he had done." (2:3)

God worked for six days and rested on the seventh. This tells us that rest is good. It's right to thank God it's Friday, because God rested.

God didn't rest because he was tired. God rested to enjoy the finished work of the first six days, which, in his words, was very good! We are wise when we do the same. We need to rest—not just because we need to recharge before another working week, which we do, but also because our good God wants us to enjoy him and keep ourselves free from the slavery of overwork (which our culture often tells us is the only way to find our identity and purpose).

So when we rest—whether it's by getting enough sleep, stopping work one day in seven, or going on holiday—we remind ourselves that we are not God, and the world doesn't depend on us.

Work Is Good

God rested, so rest is good—but it would be a mistake to think that if rest is good, work must be bad. Genesis tells us that rest and work are *both* good.

We know this because Genesis 2:3 shows God as a worker. The creation story in Genesis 1 doesn't paint a picture of work as something the almighty Creator thought was beneath him, or as something that he did as little as possible of, before creating someone else to do it. (This idea was very popular in other ancient cultures.) Genesis shows God's work as energetic and purposeful, powerful and authoritative, creative yet organised, visionary but detailed, and imaginative but still wonderfully practical. That sounds like fun! If this could leave us in any doubt that God enjoyed his work, Genesis 1 shows God sealing his work with the six-times-repeated verdict "it was good" and a resounding seventh "it was *very* good"!

God's work was good, and ours should be too. He enjoyed his work, and so should we. All of this—good rest and good work—took place in the perfect world that existed *before* the moment when sin and death invaded our story. God worked, and as we'll see shortly, God made humans to work in his very good world as part of his perfect plan.

We Were Made to Work

The author Tim Keller points out that people who cannot work, whether for physical or other reasons, quickly discover how much they *need* work in order to thrive emotionally, physically and spiritually. The next bit of the story gives us some clues as to why this is:

> "Then the LORD God formed a man from the dust of the ground and breathed into his nostrils the breath of life." (2:7)

Notice two things here.

First, we see God stooping down to the dust. Why is this significant? If you look slightly earlier in the passage, you'll see that before humans were made, "there was no one to work the ground" (v 5). That suggests that when God made humans, part of the reason was that he wanted to provide management and care for the ground. That's one of the things humans are for. And what did God make these ground-managers out of? The ground itself. We were made of the same building blocks as the thing we were created to tend. Since the beginning, then, work has been a fundamental part of us.

Second, we see God "forming" us. This is an artistic word, reminiscent of a potter carefully forming clay. God put meticulous thought into how he made us, including our likes, dislikes, abilities and personalities.

In fact, the way he uniquely formed you is one of the best indicators as to the kind of work you should do.

This short scene ends with God, face to face with the man, as he breathes into his nostrils. God exhales; we inhale. The beginning of a beautiful partnership.

We Are Called by God

I have attended many boring work ceremonies. I've also been to one that I'll never forget. My friend invited my wife and I to his retirement ceremony at the end of his service in the US Navy. It was a deeply emotional afternoon involving uniforms, flags, poetry, movement and music. Every sight and sound came together to celebrate the fact that he had been called by the most powerful nation on the planet and commissioned to the task of defending its people and their interests. What could be more meaningful than that?

According to Genesis, one answer is: being commissioned by the Creator of heaven and earth to work in his world.

> "The LORD God took the man and put him in the Garden of Eden to work it and take care of it." (2:15)

God commissions us to partner with him in creating a world where his image-bearers can flourish, and where culture and creation sing with his glory. That's what work is about—whatever it is. And that's what makes our work important.

When people ask me what work I do, I have a choice to make. I happen to work as a church pastor. I also happen to work as a surgeon. Sometimes I'll tell them one or the other, sometimes both. It's always interesting to see how different people tend to value one or the other more. But Genesis shows us that both are of equal value in God's eyes, because both are ways of taking care of the world he made.

This is also true of the different jobs within the hospital where I work. The surgeons play a crucial role in performing life-changing operations. However, the best surgeons know that their surgical expertise may come to nothing if there is no hospital kitchen team keeping the patients well-nourished so that their bodies can heal, or if there are no cleaning staff to clean the rooms and hallways to minimise the risk of the surgical wounds becoming infected. Every kind of work is important and has been given dignity by God. I love the way that Martin Luther King Jr. once put it:

> "If a man is called to be a street sweeper, he should sweep streets even as Michelangelo painted, or Beethoven composed music, or Shakespeare wrote poetry. He should sweep streets so well that all the host of heaven and

earth will pause to say: Here lived a great street sweeper who did his job well."

We Are Called to Serve

God made us to work and then gave us work to do. In Eden, that meant working the garden and taking care of it. For us today, it means anything that is part of caring for our world and the people in it, and that is helpful for their flourishing. Interestingly, money isn't mentioned in Genesis 2. This means that pay cannot be the most important thing about our work, despite what our culture may say. After all, some of the hardest work we do in life, from passing exams to raising children, does not earn us any money at all.

Genesis shows us a wonderful continuity between God's work and ours. God works by creating, and then he commissions humans to continue his work by caring for his creation. This begins a thread that runs throughout the story of the Bible, showing us how, as we work to care for this world, God is working through our work to care for his creation. He wants to care for people, and he does that through the work of people. This means our work becomes, in Martin Luther's words, the "fingers of God" in his creation and for all humanity. It doesn't get better than that!

So rest is good, and so is work. God made us to work

so that we can partner with him in his ongoing work and joy of caring for all that he has made.

What work do you do—paid or unpaid? If you can reimagine your work as something God himself has called you to and that he wants to do through you, who knows? You could spend the rest of your working life saying, “Thank God it’s Monday!”

CHAPTER 7: MARRIAGE

Getting married is about more than just the two of you.

JEZ FIELD

Have you ever had an amazing image or idea in your head that you tried to draw on paper? It might be really real and vivid and detailed in your head, but getting it into the real world is incredibly hard work and requires a lot of skill.

The Bible says that marriage is a bit like that. You probably think marriage is about two people committing to each other, and it is, but it's also about far more. Marriage puts the dramatic love relationship between Jesus and his people onto the page—except that instead of being on a page, it is acted out in a real-life flesh-and-blood relationship between a husband and a wife.

I recognise that this is a very different way of talking about marriage from most people in our society. Some say that marriage is an oppressive institution, like slavery. Others say it's a necessary evil or a way of taming men! It was reported recently that in the US, 38% of women in their twenties think that marriage is outdated; in fact, 70% of all couples under 30 choose to live together rather than get married. Fifty years ago, there was pressure on young people to get married before they lived together, but today it is exactly the opposite. We are told that people should live together first and get married later (if at all).

When *Stranger Things* star Millie Bobby Brown revealed she had got engaged at age 19, many fans were outraged. The author Freya India observed, "I see young men praised for committing, while young women are warned. We are proud of young men; we pity young women." Many young women say they feel a pressure to stay single and to not "waste" their youth by committing to a man too early in life.

So which is it? Something admirable or something outdated? A man-made custom or—as I'm about to claim—something that's actually central to the purpose of the entire universe?

The Ultimate Love Story

The idea that marriage is a picture of the relationship between Jesus and his people can be found all over the Bible, but it's probably put most clearly at the end, in the magnificent vision of Revelation:

> "I saw the Holy City, the new Jerusalem, coming
> down out of heaven from God, prepared as
> a bride beautifully dressed for her husband."
> (Revelation 21:2)

John, the writer of those words, has a vision of a wedding between a bride and her husband which lasts into eternity. In this vision, the bride is the church—that is, all followers of Jesus—and the husband is Christ. (So, if someone asks what heaven is like, one biblical answer would be: it's like a perfect marriage. Jesus is the bridegroom, and the church is the bride.)

Another Bible writer, Paul, makes a similar link between human marriage and this eternal marriage:

> "'For this reason a man will leave his father
> and mother and be united to his wife, and the
> two will become one flesh.' [Paul is quoting
> Genesis there.] This is a profound mystery—
> but I am talking about Christ and the church."
> (Ephesians 5:31-32)

What does this actually mean? Think of it this way. When a West End show goes on tour around the country, the job of the touring company is to portray the original London production. They're not allowed to reinvent the story or change the characters; their job is to represent it faithfully. In the same way, husbands and wives are playing the parts of Christ and the church. Our job is to represent these characters faithfully, not to mess around with the script. Husbands play Jesus, who lays down his life for his people to save and purify them. Wives play the church, which responds to Jesus by honouring and yielding itself to him. If we want to know how to be a good husband or wife, we need to look at Jesus and his people.

This is why we hear Jesus insist that marriage is a good and meaningful part of God's created design (Matthew 19:4-6). Marriage is a very significant part of many people's lives, but it's not just that. It matters how we approach it because it's about far more than just ourselves.

Back to the Beginning

All of these passages are built upon the foundations we read about in Genesis 2—the first mention of marriage in the Bible (and the passage Paul was quoting in those verses from Ephesians).

> "The LORD God caused the man to fall into a deep sleep; and while he was sleeping, he took one of the man's ribs and then closed up the place with flesh. Then the LORD God made a woman from the rib he had taken out of the man, and he brought her to the man.
>
> The man said, 'This is now bone of my bones and flesh of my flesh; she shall be called "woman", for she was taken out of man.'
>
> That is why a man leaves his father and mother and is united to his wife, and they become one flesh.
>
> Adam and his wife were both naked, and they felt no shame." (Genesis 2:21-25)

These words contain worlds of insight and application. Notice four things in particular.

1. Marriage involves *two* people. Not one. Not three or four. We don't have Adam, Eve, Adam's ex-girlfriend Maisie and another person they met last night in town. We have one man and one woman. That's it.

2. Marriage involves two *different* people. Adam and Eve are not the same sex. They are equal in dignity and value—notice that Eve is made from Adam's side to show that they share the same nature and purpose—but they are different.

Their body parts fit together in a way that is not true of men and men, or women with women. That is by design.

3. Marriage involves two different people *becoming one*: "That is why a man leaves his father and mother and is united to his wife" (2:24). Part of the reason for marriage is for a male and a female to find and express unity. In marriage a new household gets made: the husband and wife "leave" their parents and start something new that is intended to be permanent.

4. Marriage involves two different people becoming one, *with the potential to make more people*. Human bodies are designed to produce life: to "be fruitful and increase in number" and "fill the earth" (1:28). Not every marriage produces children, but every marriage should be open to the possibility and have the potential for it.

The Bigger Story

Each of these four truths about marriage are important, and they all have implications that put distance between how many in our society think about marriage and how the Bible describes it. For example, Christians have always believed that marriage is between one man and one woman, not a man and a man or a woman and a woman. Christians believe that sex is meant for marriage and therefore people shouldn't live with their partner outside of marriage. (If you have questions about these things, read the next chapter.)

But the Bible's picture is not just about what marriage isn't. It gives us a challenging and beautiful template for what marriage *is*—or what it can be at its best. Jesus and the church play different parts in their relationship; so do husbands and wives. Jesus and the church are committed to each other—Jesus doesn't just move in with the church and then move out if things get tricky—so human marriages should work the same way. The relationship between Christ and the church is built around self-sacrifice and submission; human marriages should be like that too.

Without Jesus, you might have thought that marriage was just some convenient social arrangement—a useful way of creating alliances between tribes or families. You might have thought that marriage was just about showing someone how much you loved them; you might have thought it was a sensible way to ensure the survival of the human species.

Marriage is indeed all of these things. But when Jesus came, something better was revealed.

I remember my youngest son's first big firework display. Until then, he'd only really seen his own family's amateur attempts at lighting rockets in the back garden. But now he saw what a real display was like! I remember looking over to see him wide-eyed in wonder, with his mouth open in an enormous smile. He was in awe of the beauty and magic of it all.

Human marriages are like rockets in the garden in comparison to the true display that Jesus reveals. When Jesus came, we saw what marriage was meant to be and we saw what love and romance really mean. He came first, his love came first, and his love for his people will last for ever. With Jesus we can say with absolute certainty, "And they all lived happily ever after."

CHAPTER 8: SEXUALITY

God invented sex for a bigger reason than you think.

ASHLEIGH HULL

I fell in love with one of my friends when I was 16. She was a girl, like me, but that wasn't a problem to me—I had no issues with the way that my sexuality seemed to work.

God did, though. I'd grown up in church, and I knew that God did not see gay relationships the same way I did. But I loved her, and she loved me too. How could that be wrong? Did God really say no to this when it made us both so happy?

To answer these questions, we need to ask some other, more fundamental questions. We need to consider why sex exists, and why humans so easily make a mess of it; what God does about that, and how we respond. That's what we're going to consider in this chapter.

The Inventor of Sex

It can be so easy to read some of the laws about sex in the Bible and think that God is squeamish about sex or doesn't like it. He says so much about who we can't sleep with—relatives, animals, people of the same sex, people we aren't married to—that it's easy to think he just doesn't want us to have sex at all.

But this is another topic where Genesis 1 – 3 is really helpful. Not only does God not dislike sex, he *invented* it!

> "So God created mankind in his own image; in the image of God he created them; male and female he created them. God blessed them and said to them, 'Be fruitful and increase in number; fill the earth and subdue it.'" (1:27-28)

God makes male and female humans, and says to them, *Make more humans! Have sex! Make babies!* God seems pretty positive about sex here.

Or turn the page to Genesis 2, where we get a second creation account—a zoomed-in version of the creation of humans. God creates someone both like and unlike

Adam—someone who is the same, who is an equal, but who is also fundamentally different—and brings her to him in the world's first marriage. "That is why a man leaves his father and mother and is united to his wife, and they become one flesh" (2:24). Sex isn't just a mechanical process for making babies. It's also part of a husband and wife becoming "one flesh". God designed sex as one of the ways that they can express and enjoy their intimate one-ness.

God made sex, he made it enjoyable, and he thinks it's great.

The Purpose of Sex

Sex exists for a very practical reason, as we've seen: making babies. And the one-flesh union that sex is a part of allows a husband and wife to stand together as they face the challenges of pregnancy, birth and parenthood. Often sex is talked about as a way of gaining pleasure for yourself, but sex is actually designed to be about *giving* yourself—both to the person beside you and to the little person who may come after you.

But sex is about even more than this important practical reality.

Sex tells a story. It is a picture of a greater reality. Think of the complementary pair of male and female—two different beings—coming together as one. It's a picture of another, greater pair: Jesus and the church. The union of Jesus and his church (or, in the language of the Old Testament, of God and his people) is a massive theme in the Bible. Sex is meant to show us this greater reality—the union that we were made for and that one day we will experience in full. Just as male and female are united in sex and marriage, so we, the church, will ultimately be united with Jesus in the new creation. We will be one with him.

So God thinks sex is great; and he designed it to tell us an even greater story.

The Misuse of Sex

But humans are complicated. We bear God's image, and our creation was called "very good" (1:31), but we are also disobedient rebels against God's rule and exiles from his presence (3:1-24). We live with twin realities: we are good, but fallen. Beautiful, but damaged. We're knocked off kilter, unbalanced, misaligned, and so we want the wrong things, or we want the right things in the wrong way. This affects everything in our lives—including sex.

We simultaneously think too much and too little of sex. Too much: that sex is necessary for a fulfilled life, and anyone who isn't having it is not a real adult or not fully enjoying life. And too little: that sex is a meaningless act, a kind of play for adults; that anything goes, as long as everyone involved is consenting. Either way, we can conclude that God's boundaries are unnecessary, either because sex is so important that it shouldn't be limited or because it doesn't matter enough to make rules about.

Instead of using sex for God's good purposes, we abuse it for ours. Instead of treasuring it within a male-female, one-flesh marriage union, we degrade it by having sex with anyone we take a fancy to: people we aren't married to, people of the same sex as us, multiple different people, or ourselves.

We misuse sex in all these ways and more. We take God's good gift and use it completely wrongly, as if we were given a new blender and tried to use it as a skateboard. It doesn't work like we want it to, and there's a lot of damage done in the process.*

The Way Out

Then Jesus comes. He steps down right into our muck and mess and pain: divorce, rape, abortion, broken trust, broken promises and broken hearts. Jesus allows himself to be completely coated with the filth of our mistakes, including the sexual ones. He lets it kill him, where it's trying to kill us.

* You might have questions about this that I don't have space to answer here—about same-sex attraction, or sex and sexuality as a whole. Keep reading, because there's good news coming; but when you've finished this chapter, head to livingout.org to hear more on all this.

And then he proves that he is who he said he is! Our sinful mess can't hold him, and our death can't keep him. Jesus rises from the grave, utterly defeating sin and pain and death in the process, and offers us his hand. We can rise with him, out of the pit and into the light of his new, resurrection life. Jesus offers us forgiveness for our mistakes, freedom from our shame and healing for our hurts. And he offers to transform us, so that we become more and more how we were originally designed to be.

That alone is glorious news. But even that is not the end of the story. One day, Jesus is going to return and make all of creation brand new, like a torn and faded painting restored to its former colour and glory. The heavens and the earth will finally be united; Jesus and his bride, the church, will be married for ever. And sex and marriage, which have been like signposts pointing to these awesome realities, will cease to exist—because when you arrive at the destination, you don't need the signposts anymore.

Sex is good, but it's pointing to something *better*. The best sex anyone could ever have on this earth is nothing more than a pale shadow of the intimacy and delight that Christians will enjoy in our eternal union with Jesus as a part of his bride, the church. That won't be a sexual union in the way human husbands and wives experience it now. It'll be something different—and something far better.

The Choice

The way that I was using sex at 16 was a misuse of God's good gift. Even though to me it seemed like a good thing, it was exploiting and distorting what God had made.

Understanding that didn't make obeying him easy. It didn't make it feel good to deny myself what I wanted. What did help was knowing Jesus himself.

In Philippians 3:8, Paul says that "everything else is worthless when compared with the infinite value of knowing Christ Jesus my Lord. For his sake I have discarded everything else, counting it all as garbage, so that I could gain Christ" (NLT). Before I really knew Jesus, that sounded like madness to me. But now, knowing him, it's the most obvious truth in the world. Everything else is worthless compared to Jesus. Being loved by him is so much better than being loved by anybody else.

So in the end, I chose Jesus. And every day I am so glad that I did! Jesus is worth having, even if having him means giving up everything else. No matter what you're looking at, Jesus is better.

What will you choose?

“People today tend to run from commitment and ‘labels’ and opt for more ‘freedom’. But this causes instability and confusion. The Bible’s way is better. It has helped me walk confidently and without fear because I know who Jesus says I am.”

LEANNE, AGED 19

CHAPTER 9: SIN

When we build our lives on things that aren't God, we end up in trouble.

JOE MACNAMARA

Shortly after my wife and I were married, she left the house one morning to go to church. She was serving and so needed to be there early. Moments after she left, she called me. "Joe, I've crashed into a parked car on the street. Can you come out?"

Thankfully, it was only a very minor scratch. As she was going off to church, I assured her that I would leave a note on the car with our contact details.

But as I went inside to get some paper, a little voice came into my head saying, "That's going to cost you a lot of money. No one saw it anyway; don't bother leaving a note." I entertained the voice for a moment before shutting it down and doing the right thing—leaving all our contact details. The owners later got in touch, and we paid for the repairs to their car.

Human beings have a history of doing lots of bad things. Some seem small, like damaging someone else's car and not telling them, while others seem much bigger. We all agree that humanity is responsible for so much evil in the world.

The question we need to ask is: why?

Although everyone agrees that there is something wrong with the world, there is a difference of opinion as to why that is. What makes us do bad things, and what is the cause of evil? Some psychologists would argue that people are basically good, and any evil behaviour comes from a person's upbringing. Maybe they were neglected, experienced trauma or were raised in poor conditions.

Those things may influence human behaviour, but they certainly don't explain everything. For starters, it still leaves a question about those who grew up well cared for, well-educated and financially stable. How do we explain it when they also do evil things?

The Bible explains this with a simple three-letter word: sin.

Sin can be controversial and is something many of us find confusing. We know the Bible says that it's bad and we shouldn't do it, but we often struggle to understand what sin actually is and why it matters so much.

It all starts in the opening pages of the Bible. Adam and Eve are described as living in the Garden of Eden, "naked and ... not ashamed" (Genesis 2:25, ESV). They were created to serve and worship God, and to rule over all created things. Then, just a chapter later, everything went wrong. They listened to the lies of the serpent, and they ate fruit from a tree that they were not supposed to eat from.

Okay—but what's the big deal? It was just a piece of fruit! Is sin simply breaking the rules that God has put in place? Well, there's far more to it than that. Let's take a closer look at Genesis chapter 3.

Why "Do as You Like" Doesn't Work

God had lovingly invited Adam and Eve to enjoy the fruit from all the trees in the garden, but he warned that there was one tree they should not eat the fruit from: "For when you eat from it you will certainly die" (2:17). This wasn't God spoiling their fun but graciously warning them. He's the author of life, and he puts boundaries in place because he knows how we will best flourish and thrive.

When I was in school, we would play football in the playground with no goals and no lines to mark out the pitch. This meant constant arguments. It was chaos! Football is most enjoyed when it is played within the boundaries it was designed with—goals, a clearly marked pitch, and a referee. Introducing order makes it more enjoyable for everyone.

In the same way, God knows how life is designed to be lived. He created it. The boundaries he puts in place—just like boundaries in a football match—enable us to enjoy life the way it is meant to be enjoyed. God doesn't warn us about sin because he loves rules but because he loves us. He wants us to live life in all its fullness.

Adam and Eve decided that they knew better than God and chose to ignore the boundaries he had put in place. Instead of trusting God, they listened to the serpent.

The Bible tells us that "the serpent was more crafty than any of the wild animals the LORD God had made" (3:1). He didn't burst onto the scene with violence or something else obviously evil, but began with a subtle question: "Did God really say, 'You must not eat from any tree in the garden'?" (3:1).

In other words, *Can you really trust God? Is he really good? Has he really said what you think?* A seed of doubt is sown. Within a few verses, this doubt has led

Adam and Eve to reject the words of God outright and disobey his good rules.

"I Know Better Than God"

But sin isn't just about doing bad things. Ultimately, it's about building your life and meaning on something other than God.

Adam and Eve were drawn into sin by the serpent's tempting offer: "You will be like God, knowing good and evil" (3:5). Instead of worshipping and serving God, they wanted to put themselves in the place of God. And that, at root, is what sin is. Rebellion against God starts with the *replacement* of God with something or someone else.

Coming back to the story about my wife and the car: why was I tempted to not leave a note? Because I'm a sinner—but more specifically because, in that particular moment, I valued saving money more than God. I wanted to not pay for the damage more than I wanted to obey God.

There is always a reason when we lie, cheat, steal, dishonour our parents, or carry out any other sin. It's because in that moment we consider something else—money, reputation, sex, comfort, popularity—to be more important than God.

From Shame to Salvation

Sin makes people feel exposed. After Adam and Eve eat the fruit, here's the first thing that happens:

> "Then the eyes of both of them were opened, and they realised they were naked." (3:7)

The serpent's promise of knowledge delivers shame and embarrassment instead. They make clothes for themselves to hide from each other, and then they try to hide from God (as if you can play hide and seek with God!). Instead of freedom, they experience fear.

Sin might look good or feel good, but it is never good for us. It always overpromises and underdelivers. It promises life but leads to death. It separates us from God, the author and source of life, and so it leads to decay, loss and death—not just physically but spiritually.

So sin is a big problem. It started with a small lie from a serpent, but it ends in disaster. Ever since that moment in the garden, all of humanity has been guilty of it. No one is perfect. This means, in the end, we are all heading for death: "The wages of sin is death" (Romans 6:23).

If the story ended there, it would be devastating. But the Bible doesn't stop at Genesis 3:13. The good news in all of this is that human sin is the very problem Jesus came into the world to fix.

He became a human being just like us, with one crucial difference: Jesus never sinned—not once. He is the only person in all of history to live a life without sin. He was perfect in every way. And then, "God made him who knew no sin to be sin for us" (2 Corinthians 5:21). Jesus died for us, in our place, tainted by everything we've done. His love for us was so great that he was willing to die so that we might be forgiven for all our sins.

Where sin brought shame, hiding and separation from God, Jesus brings forgiveness, restoration and new life with God. All we need to do is turn away from our sinful ways (repent) and put our trust in him.

> "For the wages of sin is death, but the gift of God is eternal life in Christ Jesus our Lord."
> (Romans 6:23)

"There is so much evil and temptation in the world. Sometimes I doubt myself and my beliefs because of difficult situations. I find myself asking God, 'But why?' But I know God is faithful. In uncertainty and hardship, the Bible has helped me."

NINI, AGED 15

CHAPTER 10: SUFFERING

When life is hard, God cares.

KIRSTEN HIGGINS

The tiny chapel was full to the brim as the service began. Standing at the back, I watched my grandma closely: head high, singing the hymns with zeal and passion. How did she do it? Years before, she had watched her own daughter—my mum—die of cancer in her thirties; no mother should have to face that. Another daughter was still in the trenches of her own fight with cancer, while the third battled daily with chronic fatigue while her husband dealt with the life-changing repercussions of an accident that had resulted in paralysis. Grandma had faced her own dramatic health struggles too. Now here she stood in church, singing at her husband's funeral.

There is something incredibly powerful about

watching someone who has suffered immeasurably stand up and declare the goodness of God in the face of it. I saw her do it time and time again. I spent years questioning how she could keep doing it: heralding the goodness of God whilst holding her pain.

It is normal to question why suffering exists. For some of us, it comes from our own experience of pain or that of the people close to us; for others, it comes from what we see occurring in the world around us. Sometimes it simply arises as we work out our own faith or seek to defend it to others. When we're faced with deep pain, the first thing we often cry out in response is: Why? Why this? Why me?

God's Sovereignty

As Christians, one fixed point we have is that evil was not part of God's original creation. Creation, Genesis tells us many times, was "good" (1:4, 10, 12, 18, 21, 25); in fact, it was "very good" (1:31)! There was peace, harmony, rhythm and beauty.

But God's decree to Adam and Eve was clear: "When you eat from [the tree] you will certainly die" (2:17). Take a read of Genesis 3:14-19, and you'll see that the first humans' sinful choice (as with all of our sinful choices) caused suffering in the form of enmity, pain, toil, sweat and ultimately death. Evil is not accidental. It entered the world through our sin.

Yet, although suffering exists because of our sin, that doesn't mean it is beyond God's control. God is sovereign—he is in charge of all things, and nothing happens without his permission. This can be a hard thing to consider when suffering hits us, but the truth is that God allows suffering to happen for his purposes. That does not mean that God is responsible for the evil that humans commit—we can't duck our responsibility and refuse to take ownership for the evil we do—but God allows it to happen in the same way he allows other evil things—natural things like diseases and disasters—to occur.

God's Discipline

Sometimes, although not always, God does not just allow suffering but causes it. That is clearly true in Genesis 3, where God tells Adam and Eve that their lives will now involve suffering because of what they have done. We see it in other Scriptures too. One example is the case of King David in 2 Samuel 11 – 12. David commits adultery and murder, and God punishes him for it. David suffers. This suffering is not purposeless, however. It ultimately leads David to recognise his sin and repent. In the end, his suffering produces goodness. God is not hatefully seeking vengeance on David but disciplining him for his good.

So, God sometimes causes suffering. But here are three things this does *not* mean:

- The more we suffer, the more we have sinned.
- If we are experiencing suffering, we must have done something wrong.
- If we are experiencing suffering, God must be angry with us.

If we trust in Jesus, all our sins have been cancelled (Colossians 2:14). They don't count anymore. They have been taken away because justice has been served through the death of Jesus. This means that God is not angry with us. When he does allow us to suffer, he is using it to change us and grow us. His discipline is entirely designed to draw us lovingly back into his arms.

God's Mystery

We could spend a lifetime asking "why?" about every moment of suffering in our lives. It's even tempting to use this question as a way to feel like we're fixing or controlling our pain, or at least doing something about it. You see, as humans we like to understand everything. We think that if we can just search under every rock until we completely understand the whats, whys and hows of our pain, then somehow that will help. But we can never completely understand it.

Christians are called to do something else in the midst of our pain, and that is to trust. We are invited to bring our suffering to a loving Father and trust that the God who created the world and sent his Son to die for us will ultimately bring good out of all tragedy, just as he has promised to do. We are invited to trust, and live with the mystery of it all.

This is not always easy, but it is good! The satisfaction of trusting him is like nothing else.

God's Embrace

So how do we do it? How do we trust God? By remembering that in Jesus, God entered into suffering. Jesus suffered physically as he was beaten, tortured, crucified and killed. He suffered emotionally as he was tempted, ridiculed, spat upon and shamed. He suffered spiritually as he carried the weight of every sin that has been or will be committed, and the curse that it rightly deserves (Galatians 3:13). He knows what suffering is like.

Satan exploits our suffering by whispering to us that God knows *about* our suffering, but he doesn't care—that he is a cold, hard master, observing and unmoved. But the truth is that God is close to the broken-hearted and has a special love for those who feel crushed (Psalm 34:18). I invite you today to get rid of the idea that God is unmoved by suffering! No, our suffering causes him to be greatly grieved. He knows what it is to suffer, and his response is one in which compassion and mercy flow out in abundance. His desire is to draw us to himself, like a father with a child, and to carry us into his loving embrace.

Something deeply powerful happens within us when, in the mystery of our suffering and in the depth of our weakness, we choose to fall into the embrace of our Father in heaven and the God of all comfort. If you feel weak in your suffering today, the Bible promises that God's strength is made perfect in our weakness (2 Corinthians 12:9). We don't have to suffer on our own; there is an invitation to lean on him. God's nearness is a constant that carries us in our pain and sees us through our darkest days as we look to the promise that "in all things God works for the good of those who love him" (Romans 8:28).

God's Purpose

I once heard it said that our biggest areas of pain and brokenness have the potential to be the areas in which God uses us the most. Why? Because our God is a Redeemer who takes what is broken and makes it beautiful. I'm struck that in Psalm 30:11, David writes, "You have turned for me my mourning into dancing" (ESV). He doesn't say that God has taken away his mourning and given him gladness as a replacement. He says that mourning has been *turned into* dancing: ashes have turned into beauty, and pain has turned into joy. God redeems our pain by transforming it into something else.

That doesn't mean we always have the answers we want. But it does mean God's presence is with us. And when we are in his presence, it is like healing balm to our wounds.

I cannot tell you why those members of my family have experienced the suffering they have. I cannot tell you why, despite the countless prayers of so many, we never saw their bodies healed. But God's word assures me that even if I cannot understand his mystery, I can trust his goodness. I can find comfort in his embrace, sympathy in his understanding, encouragement in his purposes, and hope in the fact that suffering is not the end.

"Asking Jesus for forgiveness is the most amazing feeling. It's understanding that you need to humble yourself and ask for forgiveness, but that God will respond with open arms full of love. It's awesomeness and peace and happiness all at once."

TIM, AGED 16

CHAPTER 11: SHAME

You don't have to hide anything from God.

DAN FEATHERSTONE

Sin makes people hide. We sin, which brings shame, which brings a terrible desire to withdraw, cover ourselves up and disappear into the bushes.

Do you know that feeling? I certainly do. If so, you are acting from the same script as all humans have done since the garden. Of all the terrible results that flowed from Adam and Eve's sin—evil, injustice, slavery and death—the one that Genesis highlights first is the exposure of their nakedness. God calls them out, and Adam responds by saying, "I heard you in the garden, and I was afraid because I was naked; so I hid" (3:10).

It's an unsurprising response to sin. Adam had been given everything by God: a beautiful garden to look after, animals to tend, creation to rule, and a wife to partner with. Yet Adam failed through his disobedience. He betrayed God for a piece of fruit. He felt shame, and rightly so.

It is natural that we do too. Shame comes from the knowledge that we have let God down through our sin and disobedience. It causes us to run and hide: hide our sin, hide from God, hide from our friends and relatives and church leaders. (Sometimes shame arises from evil things that other people have done to us, rather than things we have done ourselves. But the connection between sin and shame is always there.)

Humans, we have a problem.

The Snake-Crusher

But God has the solution. And it comes in the form of a promise—not to the man or to the woman but (bizarrely) to the serpent. God said:

> "Cursed are you above all livestock and all wild animals! You will crawl on your belly and you will eat dust all the days of your life. And I will put enmity between you and the woman, and between your offspring and hers; he will crush your head, and you will strike his heel." (3:14-15)

This is a declaration of war, and a promise of victory. There will be enmity, or hatred, between the serpent and humanity—but the day will come when an offspring of the woman (a human being) will crush the head of the serpent (Satan). What we are hearing here is the first-ever promise of God's plan to enter the world in the person of Jesus in order to destroy sin, shame, guilt and death. Jesus crushed Satan.

Back in Genesis, there were still devastating consequences to Adam and Eve's sin. They were sent out of God's presence, banished from the garden of Eden (3:23). But even in this moment of judgment, there was proof of the fact that God had not abandoned them. Aware that Adam and Eve felt exposed and ashamed in their nakedness, "the LORD God made garments of skin for Adam and his wife and clothed them" (3:21). God literally covered their exposure. It demonstrated that God was not done with humanity but longed to cover our shame once and for all.

Hope for My Shame

I find myself in the place of Adam and Eve. If God is so holy and perfect that he has to put sin out of his presence (as he does here), and if I am imperfect and prone to sin (which I am), then how can I not be filled with great shame? I don't live up to what God has called me to. Although I know that God loves me, I often let him down. I sin time and time again. Frequently I try to hide this from others. Sometimes it means I do not to want to pray or look to God because I feel ashamed of what I have done.

But Genesis 3 gives me hope. God is in the business of covering those who are exposed, honouring those who are ashamed, and saving those who sin. He promised that he would send a snake-crusher, and in the person of Jesus, that is exactly what he did.

> "For God so loved the world that he gave his one and only Son, that whoever believes in him shall not perish but have eternal life."
>
> (John 3:16)

God came into the world in Jesus, born of a woman by the power of the Holy Spirit. He lived a human life. He was hungry, got tired, experienced loss, mourned the death of a friend. He experienced temptation but stood firm in obedience to the Father. He was rejected by those he came to save: they beat him, whipped him, mocked him, spat at him, cursed him, thrust a crown of thorns on his head, stripped him and nailed him to a wooden cross.

Think about how shameful the cross was. Consider the mockery and nakedness, the spitting and taunting, the ridicule and exposure, with people gloating over his pain and gambling over his clothes. Why is that so important? Because he was carrying all the shame of all the sin that all the sinners in history have ever committed. With all the weight of that shame upon him, Jesus finally cried out, "My God, my God, why have you forsaken me?" Then he gave up his life.

But three days later, Christ was raised from the dead, defeating the curse of sin once and for all. For those of us who trust in him, our shame has now been covered with honour. Our nakedness has been clothed with resurrection life. We are no longer banished from God's presence but welcomed into his home. Just as God clothed Adam and Eve by killing an animal and using its skin, so Christ has clothed us by being killed himself.

My shame tells me, "I don't deserve Christ to do that for me". But the Bible tells me, "God demonstrates his own love for us in this: while we were still sinners, Christ died for us" (Romans 5:8). I will never deserve such a great love and such a great sacrifice. But God isn't asking me to deserve it or earn it.

I no longer have to hide. When God looks at me, he doesn't see my shameful failures but instead sees Christ's honour and perfection. He has dealt with my sin—and yours—once and for all.

The God of the Second Chance

In John 8:1-11, we read about a woman caught in adultery. Jesus is teaching in the temple courts, and the teachers of the law throw the woman before him. She must be feeling great shame. Not only has she sinned against God, but she has been caught in the act and is now being shamed in public.

The teachers expect Jesus to agree with their judgment that she should die. In some ways, they are not wrong. But Jesus doesn't speak words of judgment. Instead he looks at her accusers and says, "Let any one of you who is without sin be the first to throw a stone at her." One by one they all leave, knowing that none of them meet their own perfect standards.

Imagine you are this woman. Your worst sin has been exposed. Everyone knows about it. You are standing before Jesus, and he knows. There is no doubt that you have sinned against God. Everyone else has realised their own guilt and slunk away, leaving just you and Jesus.

How would you feel? Guilt, probably. Fear, possibly. Shame, certainly. If it were me, I would expect him to act according to what I deserve, judging me or even executing me for breaking God's law. But then Jesus—the one whom God promised would crush the head of the serpent—says those astonishing and life-giving words:

> "Neither do I condemn you ... Go now and leave your life of sin." (John 8:11)

God gives all of us a second chance (and a third, and a fourth, and a fifth). Through Christ, we are freed from all our shame and given the opportunity to leave our life of sin behind and follow Jesus into all he has for us. This is God's "amazing grace ... which saved a wretch like me"! I am no longer lost in my sin and shame but found and covered by the God who loves me.

Stop hiding! Step out of the shadows. Come and be covered by the God who takes away shame and clothes you with honour instead.

"If you believe in God, even if there are days when you don't *feel* it, the *knowledge* of his love reassures you with hope for the future. He is above all things, yet sees you and is relatable to you. No despair is too big for Jesus."

ZOË, AGED 15

CHAPTER 12: HOPE

No matter what, things are going to get better.

MARTIN SEGAL

When I was growing up, one of my favourite films was *The Lion King*. Like so many stories, it begins with everything going well. Simba the lion cub is born into a loving family and, as a young prince, is learning what it means to be king. Life is good, the land is flourishing and there is a clear sense of order and purpose... until, suddenly, everything goes wrong.

Simba's father, Mufasa, is (spoiler alert!) killed by his brother Scar, who makes himself king. Simba must run away, separated from everything he has ever known. As he grows up, he hides from his past until, with a little help, he realises he must return and fight. But when he finally reaches his homeland, what he finds is devastating. Scar hasn't just taken the throne; the entire land has been corrupted. Nothing is growing. Life has drained away. Everything is worse under the rule of the enemy.

So when Simba eventually defeats Scar and takes his rightful place as king, he doesn't just restore himself—he restores the land. Life returns, the ground flourishes and order is re-established.

Why do stories like this capture our imagination so much? I think it's because, deep down, we long for something similar to happen in our own story. We want to believe that everything sad will one day be made good. And yet, no matter how hard we try, we can't seem to make it happen! It feels like we're confronted daily by pain, loss and disappointment. Deep in the heart of every human being is the question: Will things get better?

Hope Lost?

At the end of the first three chapters of Genesis, it can be difficult to see how the story could possibly improve. Adam and Eve are removed from the garden and from God's presence. Their own relationship, once marked by love and unity, is now filled with blame and shame. And the impact doesn't stop with them. The curse of sin spreads outward and affects all of God's perfect creation.

Look at 3:16-19. The consequences of sin are cosmic: they don't just separate humans from God's presence, but they also cause work to be exhausting and frustrating, childbirth to be painful, thorns and thistles to grow instead of plants and trees. Just as in *The Lion King*, everything is corrupted.

We are still living in the fallout. You don't even have to believe in the Genesis story to see it. Every tragedy, scandal and war is a reminder that something in our world is deeply broken. And when we walk through suffering and pain in our own lives, we experience first-hand how easily sin and sorrow can drain hope away.

False Hope

To make things worse, so much of what people tell us we can hope in or find meaning from actually leads us deeper into hopelessness.

Many people turn to science and rationalism to make sense of the world, but the answer offered here is often bleak. It tells us that life is meaningless, everything is random, and there is no ultimate hope for restoration. We live, we suffer and we die.

This way of thinking flows from atheism—the belief that there is no God and that life is an accident and therefore has no ultimate purpose or meaning.

Whether we realise it or not, this worldview has deeply shaped our culture. It has bred a sense of meaninglessness, leaving people wandering aimlessly. If we are here by accident and have no purpose, then suffering is inevitable and unchangeable. Things will only continue to decline until there is nothing left.

Another answer you might hear is more optimistic but just as empty. It tells you that life has meaning and that things can get better—but only for you, and only through you. It's a dog-eat-dog world. Put yourself first. Chase your dream. Many of the success stories we celebrate are about individuals who have come from nothing and achieved everything. Entrepreneurs, athletes, celebrities: all of them are praised for working harder, being more talented and climbing higher than everyone else.

From a young age, many of us are taught to dream of fame, wealth and success. But the reality is that this hope benefits the individual while leaving everyone else unchanged. Worse still, it turns us inward. Just look around, and you can see where this path leads: greed, isolation and disappointment. Even when it "works", it rarely satisfies. The Bible is painfully clear that storing up "treasures on earth" (Matthew 6:19) ultimately leads to emptiness, because everything we cling to here will one day be lost, stolen or destroyed.

Hope Found

We live in a world marked by hopelessness, and every answer the world offers is tainted. At first glance, Genesis 3 seems to reinforce this. God pronounces curses over the serpent, Eve, Adam and even the ground itself. It appears that although life began well, all hope was lost the moment sin entered the world.

And yet, hidden within this dark chapter is a breathtaking promise. God speaks to the serpent:

> "And I will put enmity between you and the woman, and between your offspring and hers; he will crush your head, and you will strike his heel." (3:15)

This promise changes everything. You've already read in chapter 11 of this book how it changes things for us as individuals, bringing hope for our shame. But it also changes things for our world. The answer to the question "will things get better?" is a resounding yes.

This verse points to God's rescue plan—a plan he had from the very beginning. God was not surprised by sin and its effect on the world, and the moment humanity fell, he promised redemption. Genesis 3:15 is the first mention of that promise in the Bible, but it is far from the last. Throughout the Old Testament, there are over 300 promises pointing to the one who would come and make all things new.

There are three key truths here. First, the rescuer would be born of the woman. He would be fully human, entering the world in the same way every other human does. This matters because the corruption of creation came through humanity, and so the solution would also come through humanity.

The second relates to how the victory would come. The serpent would strike his heel, but the promised one would crush the serpent's head. At the cross, Jesus endured the bite of the enemy. What looked like defeat was actually God's rescue plan unfolding. Like Simba, Jesus confronted the enemy and won.

And the third is that there is hope for the whole of creation here, not just individual human beings. We've seen how sin touches everything; Romans 8:22 talks about the whole of creation "groaning as in the pains of childbirth". But hope touches everything too, and hope gets the last word. Jesus brings forgiveness to humans, but he is also bringing liberation to the whole of creation.

Through his death and resurrection, he has undone the corruption that entered the world through sin. We don't see the results yet, but we will. One day, Jesus will return, and God's rescue plan will be seen in its fullness. Creation will be restored. Deserts will become fruitful. Life will flourish again. Or, as the Christmas carol *Joy to the World* puts it:

"No more shall sins and sorrows grow,
Nor thorns infest the ground.
He comes to make his blessings flow
Far as the curse is found."

The hope of the Christian faith is not that life will be easy but that suffering and sorrow will not have the final say. Through Jesus Christ, God has made a way for things to get better. We live now with confidence and expectation, eagerly awaiting the day when Jesus returns and fully establishes his kingdom—redeeming all of creation for his glory.

"Looking back now, I can see that even when I didn't really know who God was, he was already working in my life. I've come to know that God is real, personal, and way more loving than I ever expected. There's so much more to learn and grow in, but I'm super grateful for how far Jesus has already brought me."

GEORGE, AGED 17

Space for notes:

About the authors

This book was written in collaboration with Newday Generation UK, which organises Newday Festival, a summer gathering for 12-18s.

Taylor Bentliff works in Christian media and serves on the leadership team at Newday. She has a massive herbal tea collection and a French bulldog called Mabel.

Katherine Brown became a Christian at drama school and now works for the Evangelical Alliance exploring the question "What does it mean to be human?"

Jez Field lives in East Sussex, is married to Amy and has three sons who compete against him at every sport and game. He's slowly coming to accept that his boys are faster, stronger and smarter than him.

Stu Gibbs leads the team at Newday Festival and is starting a new church called Redemption London. His primary strength is eating jelly babies.

Kirsten Higgins lives in Ipswich, where she has been leading her church youth team for nine years. She's a coffee and fitness enthusiast, though lately this looks more like downing the coffee and chasing a toddler!

Adrian Holloway is a church pastor who has been following Jesus since 1985! He's married to Julia, and they have four children. He's also the author of two books for teens called *The Shock of Your Life* and *Aftershock*.

Ashleigh Hull has only ever broken one bone—her brother's collarbone. She's prouder of this than she should be. She's a youth leader and a part of Living Out, a group of same-sex-attracted Christians who help people talk about faith and sexuality.

Dan Featherstone is married to Nikki and has two boys, Joseph and Elijah. He's part of the leadership team at Beacon Church Brixton in south London and is passionate about the word of God! He also works as a firefighter.

Joe Macnamara is the lead pastor at King's Church London. He became a Christian at a youth event when he was 15 and has been passionate about telling people about Jesus ever since!

Mbonisi Malaba is a Zimbabwean living in Kenya with his wife and teenage children. He works part-time as a surgeon and part-time as an elder at OneTribe church. He loves to run in Nairobi's stunning forests!

Martin Segal lives in Canterbury with his wife, Kathryn, and two daughters, Annabeth and Millie. He leads the eldership team at The City Church Canterbury and can do a pretty impressive Donald Duck impression.

Andrew Wilson is the teaching pastor at King's Church London and has written several award-winning books. He lives with his wife and three kids in Eastbourne on the south coast of the UK.

And not forgetting **Ollie, Dan, Grace, Leanne, Nini, Tim, Zoë** and **George,** who each contributed a little slice of their stories.

newdaygeneration.org

About Newday

Newday Generation UK is a charity that exists to help the church reach and disciple the next generation.

Newday Festival is one of the largest Christian events for young people that take place in the UK each year. Thousands of young people descend on the Norfolk Showground, travelling from all over the UK and Europe to discover and worship God, camp out together and soak in the summer festival feeling, leaving Newday further along in their relationship with Jesus.

Youth Culture equips those involved in reaching and discipling young people, including youth leaders, parents, professionals and church leaders. The annual Youth Culture Conference aims to discuss some of the biggest challenges facing young people today with expert speakers and interviews. The annual Youth Culture Retreat brings youth leaders together to spend a weekend receiving teaching and spiritual refreshment before returning to their local churches.

BIBLICAL | RELEVANT | ACCESSIBLE

At The Good Book Company, we are dedicated to helping Christians and local churches grow. We believe that God's growth process always starts with hearing clearly what he has said to us through his timeless word—the Bible.

Ever since we opened our doors in 1991, we have been striving to produce Bible-based resources that bring glory to God. We have grown to become an international provider of user-friendly resources to the Christian community, with believers of all backgrounds and denominations using our books, Bible studies, devotionals, evangelistic resources, and DVD-based courses.

We want to equip ordinary Christians to live for Christ day by day, and churches to grow in their knowledge of God, their love for one another, and the effectiveness of their outreach.

Call us for a discussion of your needs or visit one of our local websites for more information on the resources and services we provide.

Your friends at The Good Book Company

thegoodbook.com | thegoodbook.co.uk
thegoodbook.com.au | thegoodbook.co.nz